The Root Of All Evil

Leo Tolstoy

Kessinger Publishing's Rare Reprints

Thousands of Scarce and Hard-to-Find Books on These and other Subjects!

- Americana
- Ancient Mysteries
- Animals
- Anthropology
- Architecture
- Arts
- Astrology
- Bibliographies
- Biographies & Memoirs
- Body, Mind & Spirit
- Business & Investing
- Children & Young Adult
- Collectibles
- Comparative Religions
- Crafts & Hobbies
- Earth Sciences
- Education
- Ephemera
- Fiction
- Folklore
- Geography
- Health & Diet
- History
- Hobbies & Leisure
- Humor
- Illustrated Books
- Language & Culture
- Law
- Life Sciences
- Literature
- Medicine & Pharmacy
- Metaphysical
- Music
- Mystery & Crime
- Mythology
- Natural History
- Outdoor & Nature
- Philosophy
- Poetry
- Political Science
- Science
- Psychiatry & Psychology
- Reference
- Religion & Spiritualism
- Rhetoric
- Sacred Books
- Science Fiction
- Science & Technology
- Self-Help
- Social Sciences
- Symbolism
- Theatre & Drama
- Theology
- Travel & Explorations
- War & Military
- Women
- Yoga
- *Plus Much More!*

**We kindly invite you to view our catalog list at:
http://www.kessinger.net**

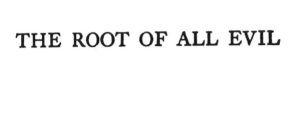

THE ROOT OF ALL EVIL

DRAMATIS PERSONÆ

AKULINA: an old woman of seventy, still hale and hearty, serious-minded, a member of the "Old Believers."

MIKHAÏLA: her son, thirty-five, passionate, conceited, boastful, strong.

MARFA: her daughter-in-law, thirty-two, querulous, talks fast and much.

PARASHKA: ten-year-old daughter of Marfa and Mikhaïla.

TARÁS: Assistant Village Policeman: fifty years old, solemn, speaks slowly, pompous.

A TRAMP: forty years old, tricky, shabby, lays down the law: when drunk his speech is generally unconstrained.

IGNÁT: forty years old, fond of buffoonery, jolly, stupid.

A NEIGHBOR: forty, officious.

THE ROOT OF ALL EVIL

A Comedy

(1910)

ACT ONE

Autumn. An Izbá with lumber-room

Scene I

Old Akulina *spinning;* Marfa *the housewife making bread; the little girl,* Parashka, *rocking the cradle*

Marfa. Oh, my heart is full of evil forebodings. Why are they gone so long? Just as t'other day when he went with the wood. He drank up half of it and it's all my fault!

Akulina. Why look for trouble? It's still early. It's a long way. Even while . . .

Marfa. Early! I should say so. Akimuitch is back already and he started long after my man did and there's no sign of my man at all. It's a wretched life, a wretched life and no joy in it.

Akulina. Akimuitch had sold his in advance but your man had to find a customer.

Marfa. There'd be no cause to worry if he had gone alone, but he took Ignat with him and when he's with that broad-snouted dog—the Lord forgive me!—there's no good in it: as sure as fate he gets drunk. All day long, it's work, work. All comes on me. If only there was something good to look forward to. But how much pleasure is there in drudging from morning till night!

(*The door opens. Enter* Taras *and a ragged* Tramp)

SCENE II

The Same, TARAS *and* THE TRAMP

TARAS. Good afternoon to you! Here, I've brought you someone who wants lodging for the night.

TRAMP [1] (*bowing*). My respects to the masters of the house.

MARFA. Why do you keep saddling them on us all the time? We had one over night last Wednesday. You always take us, yes, you take us. You might have gone to Stepanida's. They haven't any young ones. It's enough for me to look after my own. And here you're always coming to us, yes to us.

• TARAS. Everyone takes 'em in turn.

MARFA. "In turn," you say. But I have children and my man's away.

TARAS. Let him spend the night. He won't do any harm.

AKULINA (*to the* TRAMP). Come right in and sit down; we'll look after you.

THE TRAMP. Thank you. I'd like a bite of something if it's possible.

MARFA. Before he looks round he wants something to eat—first thing! Come now, haven't you been begging all through the village?

THE TRAMP (*with a sigh*). That ain't my custom, being what I am. But as I didn't bring along no pervisions of my own . . .

(AKULINA *rises, gets some bread, breaks off a piece and hands it to the Tramp*)

THE TRAMP (*takes the piece of bread*). Merci! (*Sits on a trestle and munches greedily.*)

TARAS. But where is Mikhaïla?

[1] Tramps were quartered at the izbas in turn under the direction of the Village Authorities.

MARFA. He went to town with his hay. He ought to be back, but there's no sign of him. I keep thinking something's happened to him.

TARAS. What could have happened to him?

MARFA. What a question! No good, you may be sure; nothin' but bad. When he's away from home, he don't bother about a single thing. I expect when he does come, he'll be drunk.

AKULINA (*sits at the distaff, to* TARAS, *pointing to* MARFA). She can't never hold her tongue. This is what I say: women like her worry about everything.

MARFA. If he was alone, there wouldn't be nothing to worry about. But he and Ignat went off together.

TARAS (*smiles*). Well, Ignat Ivanuitch is always ready to take a drop too much; that's true.

AKULINA. He knows Ignat, don't he? Ignat's accountable for himself, ain't he, and he for himself.

MARFA. It's all right for you to talk, *mátushka*. But his debauchery is up to here (*indicating her throat*). When he's sober, I say no ill of him; but when he's drunk you· yourself know what he's like. If I say a word, there's trouble.

TARAS. You women are all alike. A fellow takes a drop too much. Well, suppose he does? Let him swagger around, then sleep it off; it'll come out all right in the end. But you women are always nagging.

MARFA. Have your own way. When he's drunk, everything's wrong.

TARAS. But you see you ought to have some reason about it. We men can't help drinking too much once in a while. Your business is in the house,—woman's work but we men can't help it—in doing business or meeting friends. Now if we take a drink, sure there's no harm in it.

MARFA. Yes, it's all right for you to talk, but it's tough on we women. Oh, it's tough! If you men could be hitched to our job for a week, you'd have a different story to tell. Kneadin' dough and cookin' and bakin' and spinnin' and weavin' and the cattle and every kind of work beside washin', dressin' and feedin' empty-bellied kids—it all falls on we women; but if things don't suit him to a t, specially when he's drunk, that's another story. Oh, the life of we women. . . .

THE TRAMP (*Stopping his munching*). That's right; it's the root of all evil;—I mean, all the cutostraphes of life comes from alcolic beverages.

TARAS. Probably that's what knocked you out too!

THE TRAMP. May be 't did and may be 't didn't; yet I've suffered from it;—I might have had a very different career in life, if 't hadn't been for it.

TARAS. Well, to my mind, if you drinks a reasonable amount, there ain't the least harm in it.

THE TRAMP. Well I'll say this much—it has such a power of inertia in it that it can wholly ruin a man.

MARFA. *I* say: you hustle and do your level best and the only reward you get for it 's to be ballyragged and beaten like a dog.

THE TRAMP. Moreover, there are men, that is, some persons who so completely lose their reasoning faculties that they indulge in behavior absolutely mischievous.[2] As long as he don't drink he won't take nothing that don't belong to him, even if you give him a chance at it, but as soon as he's under the influence of liquor he appropr'ates whatever comes within his reach. And how often he gets flogged and put into jail! When I steer clear of drink, I'm perfectly honest and honorable, but as soon as I get to drinking—I mean . . . as soon as such a person gets to drinking, he will grab whatever he can lay his hands on.

AKULINA. Well, it seems to me it all depends on the man himself.

THE TRAMP. That may be so if the man is well, but it's a kind o' disease.

TARAS. Disease! Nonsense! Thrash him as he deserves and this disease of yours would go away lively.— Good bye for now.

---

[2] Postupki sovsyem nyesootvyetstvuyushchiye. The TRAMP uses words which would have delighted Dr. Johnson; while the muzhiki talk in a crisp Boeotian dialect not always easy to render.—TR.

SCENE III

The Same, without TARAS

(MARFA *wipes her hands and starts to go out.*)

AKULINA (*Looks at the* TRAMP, *sees that he has eaten up the bread*). Marfa, oh Marfa, cut him off some more.

MARFA. For him? the idea! I've got to see to the samovár.   (*Exit.*)

SCENE IV

The Same, without MARFA

(AKULINA *gets up, goes to the table, takes the bread, cuts off a thick slice and gives it to the* TRAMP)

THE TRAMP. Merci. I've got a mighty good appetite.

AKULINA. Have you a trade?

THE TRAMP. *I!* I *was* a machinist.

AKULINA. Tell me, did you earn much?

THE TRAMP. Sometimes fifty, sometimes seventy.

AKULINA. That's a good bit! How did you get down an' out?

THE TRAMP. Down and out! I'm not the only one. I got knocked out because in such times as these it is impossible for an honest man to make a living.

SCENE V

The Same, and MARFA

MARFA (*Bringing the samovar*). Lord! No doubt, he'll come home drunk. I feel it in my bones.

AKULINA. Sure he wouldn't go on a spree!

MARFA. If 't ain't one thing, it's another. It's nothin' but work, work—kneedin' and bakin' and cookin' and spinnin' and weavin' and the cattle—everything on me.

(*A cry from the cradle.*)   Parashka, rock the little one.
O what a life a woman's is! And when the man's drunk,
there ain't nothin' right. . . . Say a word that don't suit
him . . .

AKULINA (*Starts to make the tea*). This is the last
of the tea. Did you remind him to bring some?

MARFA. I did. He promised to bring it. See him
bring it! Does he ever think about his home? (*Sets
the samovár on the table. THE TRAMP moves away
from it.*)

AKULINA. Now what made you leave the table? We're
going to drink tea.

THE TRAMP. I tender my thanks for your kind-hearted
hospitality. (*Throws away his tsigarka*[3] *and goes back
to the table.*)

MARFA. What sort of man be you anyway—peasant
or what?

THE TRAMP. I belong neither to the peasantry, mother,
nor to the nobility, but to the two-edged class.

MARFA. What do you mean by that? (*Hands him a
cup.*)

THE TRAMP. Merci.—I mean my father was a Polish
count, tho there were many others as well as him and
I had also two mothers. Gener'ly speaking my biography
is somewhat of a puzzle.

AKULINA. O Lord! How was that?

THE TRAMP. My mother was dissolute in her life; I
mean she was polygamous. And the fathers of her children were all kinds. And I had two mothers for the
reason that my real mother managed to get rid of me
when I was at a tender age. The dvornik's wife seems
to have had a compassionate heart and undertook to
bring me up.[4]

MARFA. Have another cup.—D'y' have any schoolin'?

THE TRAMP. My education was also haphazard. My
mother—not my real mother but the one who adopted
me—put me to blacksmithing. The blacksmith, you see,

---

[3] *Tsigarka:* a cigaret rolled from a bit of newspaper or the
like; it is also called a *dog's leg* or a *sheep's horn.*—TR.

[4] In the original manuscript only. Afterwards expunged.—Russian Editor's Note.

was my first perdagog and his perdagogy was confined
to this: that the said blacksmith used to pound me,
so that he did not pound his anvil so often's my unfor-
tunate head. Nevertheless, however much he pounded
me he could not deprive me of my talent. Then I fell
into the hands of a locksmith. And there I was appre-
ciated and accomplished something—I became a first-
class artizan. I made the acquaintance of edicated men
and entered a faction. I was enabled to acquire an
intellectual vocabulary. And my life might of been
quite superior as I was gifted with colossial talents.

AKULINA. That must be so!

THE TRAMP. And dusaster came—the despotic burden
of pop'lar life, and I got into jail, I mean into diprivation
of my liberty.

MARFA. What was that for?

THE TRAMP. For our rights.

MARFA. What on earth do you mean—"for our
rights"? What kind of rights?

THE TRAMP. What kind of rights? Why, the rights
that would prevent the *bourjwar* from eternally idling
away their time and permit the hard-working proletary
to receive a recompense for his labors.

AKULINA. You mean, possess the land?

THE TRAMP. Certingly I do. It's all included in the
argonomic question.

AKULINA. May God and the Tsáritsa of Heaven grant
it! It's getting powerfully overcrowded. But what are
you going to do now?

THE TRAMP. What now? Now I'm on my way to
Moscow. I'll hire out to some exploiter. What's the
use? I give it up. I'll say: "any work, only take me!"

AKULINA. Come now, have some more tea.

THE TRAMP. I thank you, I should say merci. (*Noise
and voices in the shed.*)

AKULINA. Here's Mikhaïla—just in time for tea.

MARFA (*rises*). Oh, my grief! With Ignat! Drunk,
of course! (MIKHAÏLA *and* IGNAT, *both drunk, come
staggering in.*)

SCENE VI

The Same, MIKHAÏLA *and* IGNÁT

IGNAT. Good af'ernoon to y'all! (*Makes the sign of the Cross to the ikon.*) Here we are,—powerful yard!⁵ jus' in time for samovár. We go to shursh—servis all over; come into dinner, ever'thing ate up, we go to wine-shop an' there 't's all right. Ha, ha, ha. You've got tea f'r us, we got liquor f'r you. Z'at's fair, ain't it? (*Laughs.*)

MIKHAILA. Where d'ye find this dude? (*Pulls a bottle out of the bosom of his coat and stands it on the table.*) Bring some cups.

AKULINA. Tell me, did you have a good trip?

IGNAT. Couldn't ha' been better, powerful yard, and we had a drink or two and we got drunk and we've brought some home with us.

MIKHAILA (*Fills cups, offers his mother one and another to* THE VAGRANT). Here you, have a drink.

THE TRAMP (*Accepts the cup*). I offer you my heart-felt gratitude. To your health! (*Drains the cup.*)

IGNAT. Goo' boy! How he swills it down, powerful yard! When one's hungry like zhat, I espec' makes nerves tingle. (*Fills up the cup again.*)

THE TRAMP (*Drinks*). I wish you success in all your enterprises.

AKULINA. Did you sell out for a good price?

IGNAT. Goo' price or bad, we drank it all up,—power-ful yard!—Ain' 'at so, Mikhaila?

MIKHAILA. Cer-certainly 't is. Why look at it twice? S'long 's we live, le's ge' drunk.

MARFA. And you brag about it; do you? It's all wrong. There's nothing to eat in the house. And here you are at it!

MIKHAILA (*threateningly*). Marfa!

MARFA. Why yell "Marfa"? I know I'm Marfa. Akh, I wish I'd never laid eyes on you, you scoundrel.

MIKHAILA. Marfa, look out!

⁵Yadryona palka, literally, sound or husky stick.

MARFA. Look out nothing! Why should I look out?

MIKHAILA. Fill up the cups; pass them to the guests.

MARFA. Tfu! goggle-eyed cur! And I don't want to speak to you!

MIKHAILA. You don't? Oh you hag, you slut! What's 'at you're shaying?

MARFA (*Rocks the cradle; the children in terror run to her*). What was I saying? I was saying that I didn't want to speak to you, and that's the end of it.

MIKHAILA. You've forgotten, have you? (*Staggers from the table, gives her a blow on the head, knocks off her kerchief.*) There's one for y'!

MARFA. O-o-oh! (*In tears runs to the door.*)

MIKHAILA. You won't get off, you rotten carcass you! (*Rushes at her.*)

THE TRAMP (*Springs from behind the table and seizes* MIKHAILA *by the arm*). You haven't the slightest right to do that.

MIKHAILA (*Stops short and gazes at* THE TRAMP *in astonishment*). Say, do you want to get a thrashing?

THE TRAMP. You have no right at all to inflict insults on the feminine sect.

MIKHAILA. Oh you son of a bitch: do you see this? (*Shows his fist.*)

THE TRAMP. I will not permit exploitation to be applied to the feminine sect.

MIKHAILA. I'll apply such an exploitation to you that you'll go head over heels . . . .

THE TRAMP. All right, strike. Why don't you strike? Strike, I say! (*Offers his face.*)

MIKHAILA (*Shrugs his shoulders and spreads his hands out*). Well now, how can I do it?

THE TRAMP. I say: Strike!

MIKHAILA. Well, you certainly are a queer chap, now I look at you. (*Drops his hand and shakes his head.*)

IGNAT (*to the* TRAMP). 'S evident at once-t you're a woman-chaser—powerful yard!

THE TRAMP. I stand for the right.

MIKHAILA (*goes to the table, breathing heavily, to* MARFA). Set up a fat candle on account of him. If 't hadn't a-been f'r him, I'd 'a' smashed y' into bits.

MARFA. What else is to be expected of you? Here I word hard all my days, cookin' and bakin' and then . . .

MIKHAILA. Now that'll do, that'll do. (*Offers liquor to the* TRAMP.) Take a drink!—(*To his wife.*) Let up on that drivel, you! You won't let me have my little fun! Here's the money, ta' care of it: two bills o' three rubles and here's a couple o' twenty-kopek pieces besides.

AKULINA. How about the tea 'n' the sugar I asked you to get?

MIKHAILA (*takes a package out of his pocket and hands it to his wife.* MARFA *seizes the money and goes to the lumber-room, silently rearranging her kerchief*). Whaz stupid folks these women is! (*He again offers liquor to the* TRAMP). Here, have anuzzer drink!

THE TRAMP (*declines it*). Drink it yourself.

MIKHAILA. Now, no puttin' on airs!

THE TRAMP (*drinks*). Good fortune attend you!

IGNAT (*to the* TRAMP). I s'pec' you've seen something of life in your day! Okh, zat's a fine *bonjourka* you've got on y'! A nirishtocratic *bonjourka*! Now, where zh' get one like zhat? (*He points to his ragged jacket.*) Don't get it mended: it's all right ash 't is. I mean, 't 's reached a good ol' age. Well, what diff'rence 's make? 'f I had one like that, all th' women'd be in love wiz me too! (*To* MARFA.) That's th' truth, ain't it?

AKULINA. It's mean, Ivánuitch, to ridicule a man you've never seen before.

THE TRAMP. It's only uneducatedness!

IGNAT. Y' see, I like him. Have a drink! (*Proffering him more liquor,* THE TRAMP *drinks.*)

AKULINA. You yourself said, "it's the root of all evil," and that you went to jail on account of it.

MIKHAILA. What d'y' go to jail for?

THE TRAMP (*Very tipsy*). I shuffered from expropriation.

MIKHAILA. How was that?

THE TRAMP. This was 'e way: went to him, to a pot-bellied man. "Hand over y'r money," we say, "or elsh' thish'—a levolver. He wrigglesh. Takesh out two-thousan' two-hunnerd rublesh.

AKULINA. O Lord!

THE TRAMP. We only wanted to do wha' was right—to dishpose of th' sum. Zembrikof wash boss of zhe job. They pounched down on us—thoshe crows. There we were under guard; they shut us up in jail.

IGNAT. And they took away the money?

THE TRAMP. Sure they did. Only they couldn't prove it on me. The Prokuror said thish to me in Court: "You stole the money," says he and I answer back: "Thieves steal money," s'ys I, "but we accomplished expropriation for the Party." An' so he hadn't anything 'ansher me. He looked zis way an' zat way but he couldn't ansher me. "Take him to jail," shays he, that means I was shut up from my free life.

IGNAT (*to* MIKHAILA). 's a clever chap, this rascal. Smar' fella'. (*Fills up the* TRAMP's *cup.*) Drink, you skunk!

AKULINA. Tfu! You talk vulgar, you do.

IGNAT. That's not obshene? jus' a shaying I invented; Dirty skunk! To y'r health, bábushka!

(MARFA *enters; standing by the table she pours tea.*)

MIKHAILA. Well. Now, thash' all right. Nothin' to get mad about. I shay, thanksh to him. And as f'r you, Marfa, I have a high respec' f'r you. (*To the* TRAMP) What's you think about it? (*Hugs* MARFA.) I have a high respec' for my old woman, jus' a high respec'. My ol' woman, on my word, 's firsht class. Catch me swappin' her off f'r any other one!

IGNAT. Thash' good. Babushka Akulina, have a drink. I stand treat.

THE TRAMP. That represents the force of enershy. A minute ago ever'one was melancholy and now 't 's nothin' but good sheer—a friendly state o' mind. Bábushka, I sherish affection for you and for all people. Dealy-beloved brer'en! (*Sings a revolutionary song.*)

MIKHAILA. He feels the effect of it 'cause he was starved.

Curtain.

ACT TWO

(The Same Cottage. Morning)

Scene I

Marfa *and* Akulina. (Mikhaïla *asleep*)

Marfa (*carries an ax*). Must go and chop up wood.
Akulina (*with a bucket*). He'd a' given you a drub-
bing last evenin', if it hadn't a-been for that man. But
he's not to be seen. Can he 'a' gone? 't must be he's
gone. (*They go out one after the other.*)

Scene II

Mikhaïla *alone*

Mikhaila (*clambers down from oven*). Seems to me
that dear little Sun's rather high. (*Stands up, gets into
his boots.*) She an' the old mother must have gone for
water. My head aches, oh, how it aches. I'll swear off!
Henceforth the devils may drink it! (*Prays to God,
washes his face and hands.*) Must go and harness up.
(Marfa *enters with faggots.*)

Scene III

Mikhaïla *and* Marfa

Marfa. So yesterday evening's tramp 's gone, has he?
Mikhaila. He must 'a' gone—'s not to be seen.
Marfa. Well, God be with him. But he seemed like
a clever man.
Mikhaila. 'Cause he stuck up for you?
Marfa. What difference does that make to me?

(MIKHAILA *completes his toilet.*) I s'pose you put away the tea and sugar you brought last evening, didn't you?
MIKHAILA. I thought you took them.
(*Enter* AKULINA *with the bucket*)

SCENE IV

The Same, and AKULINA

MARFA (*to the old woman*). Matushka, did you take the parcel?
AKULINA. I don't know nothing about it.
MIKHAILA. I left it by the window yesterday afternoon.
AKULINA. Oh, so you did—I saw you.
MARFA. Where can it be? (*They all search.*)
AKULINA. Just think, what a crime! (*A* NEIGHBOR *enters.*)

SCENE V

The Same, and the NEIGHBOR

NEIGHBOR. What do you say, Tikhonuitch,[1] shall we go after our wood, what?
MIKHAILA. Well, why not? I'll hitch up after a bit.— You see we've lost something.
NEIGHBOR. Tha' so? What is it?
MARFA. Why my man brought a package from town yesterday afternoon: tea, sugar, he laid it down by the window. I neglected to put it away: now it's lost— can't find it nowhere.
MIKHAILA. We're laying the sin on a tramp: he spent the night there.
THE NEIGHBOR. What kind of a tramp?
MARFA. A lean, unshaven fellow.
MIKHAILA. Wore a ragged pinzhachishka.[2]
NEIGHBOR. Bushy-haired? hooked nose?

---

[1] Mikhaïla Tikhónuitch.
[2] Little *pea jacket.*

MIKHAILA. Why, yes.

NEIGHBOR. I just met him, wondered who he was—
he was stepping along so fast.

MIKHAILA. That was the one, sure. Did you meet him
fur from here?

NEIGHBOR. He hadn't reached the bridge, I think.

MIKHAILA (*Seizes his cap and hurriedly exit with the*
NEIGHBOR). We must overtake him. That's the rascal—
he's the one!

SCENE VI

The Same, without MIKHAÏLA *and the* NEIGHBOR.

MARFA. Okh, the sin of it, the sin of it! No question
he done it.

AKULINA. But may be he didn't. One time—twenty
years ago 't was—in the same way they charged a man
with stealing a horse. A crowd collected: one said how
he'd seen him take it: another told how he had seen
him leading it off. And the nag was piebald, my uncle's,
easily known. The crowd kept growing, they started a
search and found a fellow in the woods—the very one!
" 'twas you," they says. He swears, he calls God to wit-
ness that it wasn't. "Why even look at him," says they?
The women declared he done it. He said something
saucy. Yegor Lapushkin—he's dead—a hot-tempered
muzhik he was, he couldn't stand it, he gave him one in
the snout. " 'twas you," says he. He struck him again.
The others 'tacked him: they went for him with sticks
and beat him to death. Next day they caught the real
thief. And all the time he wasn't the thief at all; he was
only in the woods after faggots.

MARFA. 'Tis a fact, one might make a mistake. Though
he's down and out one can see he's a good man.

AKULINA. Yes, he's terrible low down and 't 's no use
punishing such a fellow.

MARFA. What's that noise! I b'lieve they've got him.

(*Into the room come* MIKHAILA, *the* NEIGHBOR, *then an
old man, and a youth, shoving the* TRAMP *of the pre-
vious afternoon.*)

SCENE VI

The Same, MIKHAÏLA, NEIGHBOR, OLD MAN, YOUTH
and the TRAMP

MIKHAILA (*holds in his hands the parcel of tea and sugar. To his wife, in great excitement*). We found the goods on him, in his breeches. The dirty thief.

AKULINA (*to* MARFA). He's the very one! . . . poor fellow. He is hanging his head!

MARFA. Evidently he's the thief. He meant himself when he said a man always took whatever he happened to lay his hands on if he had been drinking.

THE TRAMP. I'm no thief. I'm an expropriator. I'm a worker—I have to live. You can't understand. Do what you please.

THE NEIGHBOR. Take him to the Stárosta or straight to the police.

THE TRAMP. I say, do whatever you please. I'm not afraid of any thing and I'm willing to suffer for my convictions. If only you were people of culture, you would be able to understand. . . .

MARFA (*to her Husband*). Better let him go in God's name. We've got the stuff back. Better let him go and not put a sin on us.

MIKHAILA (*repeating his wife's words*). "A sin!" You'd teach us, hey! Perhaps we don't know what to do without your meddlin'!

MARFA. I only say I'd let him off . . .

MIKHAILA. "Let him off!" Perhaps we don't know what to do without you! Well, you're a fool. "Let him off!" Whether he gets off or not, I have a word for him so he'll feel it. (*To the* TRAMP) Now you listen, *moosyé,* to what I want to say to you. Now though you are in a low down condition, yet you have done very wrong. Any one else would have given you a sound cudgelling, yes and handed you over to the police besides; but this is what I will say. You did wrong, about as wrong's could be. Only you are in a terrible low condition and I don't want to be too rough on you. (*He hesitates: all are silent.—Solemnly*) God go with you

and don't do such a thing again. (*Looks at his wife.*)
And you want to teach me!

THE NEIGHBOR. It's no use, Mikhaila. O it's no use!
you only encourage them . . .

MIKHAILA (*still holds the package in his hand*). Use
or no use, it's my affair. (*To his wife*) And you want
to teach me! (*Hesitates, looking at the package: then
deliberately gives it to the* TRAMP, *glancing at his wife.*)
And take this along; you'll have tea to drink on the road.
(*To his wife*) And you want to teach me! Get you
gone, I said, get you gone! Make no words about it.

THE TRAMP (*takes the package. A silence.*) You
think I don't comprehend. (*His voice trembles.*) I
comprehend absolutely. If you had licked me like a dog,
it would have been easier for me. Perhaps I don't comprehend what I am! I am a scoundrel, that is, a degen-
erate, that is. Forgive me, for Christ's sake! (*With a
sob, he throws the tea and sugar on the table and exit
swiftly.*)

SCENE VII

The Same, without the TRAMP

MARFA. Thank goodness, he didn't take 'em, else there
wouldn't 'a' been any for our breakfast.

MIKHAILA (*to his wife*). And you wanted to teach
me!

NEIGHBOR. Akh, he cried, poor fellow!

AKULINA. Indeed he was a real man!

Curtain

March 29, 1910. Yasnaya Polyana.
Middle of June, 1910. Meshcherskoyé. Moscow Gubernii.
In the Spring of 1910, at V. G. Chertkóf's estate, Telyatenki,
his son, V. V. Chertkóf, and some young friends, boys of the neigh-
borhood, were getting up amateur theatricals. Among other pieces
"Pyervuii Vinokur" ("The First Distiller") was staged. Lyof
Nikolayevitch was much interested in these plays and the idea
occurred to him to write a short drama for the Telyatenki theater.
In this way the Comedy, "Ot nyeï Vsyé Káchestva" ("The Root
of all Evil"; literally "From her all qualities") was created:—
Russian Editors' Note.

This is the end of this publication.

Any remaining blank pages are for our book binding requirements and are blank on purpose.

To search thousands of interesting publications like this one, please remember to visit our website at:

http://www.kessinger.net

www.ingramcontent.com/pod-product-compliance
Lightning Source LLC
LaVergne TN
LVHW091941060326
832903LV00043B/15